For Nas

Almost an Animal Alphabet

Text and Illustrations © Katie Viggers 2010

First published in Great Britain by Eightbear Press

Published by POW!

a division of powerHouse Packaging & Supply, Inc.

Library of Congress Control Number: 2013934868

37 Main Street, Brooklyn, NY 11201-1021
info@bookPOW.com
www.bookPOW.com
www.powerHousebooks.com
www.powerHousepackaging.com

ISBN: 978-1-57687-643-5

Book design by Katie Viggers

10 9 8 7 6 5 4 3

Printed in Malaysia

Almost an Animal Alphabet

By Katie Viggers

A is for Anteater aarrgh and ants

B is for bears

polar

black
(Asian)

sun

spectacled

bamboo

brown

black
(North American)

sloth

panda

C is for

Cat

Tyrannosaurus rex

Triceratops

dinosaur

Stegosaurus

Pterodactyl

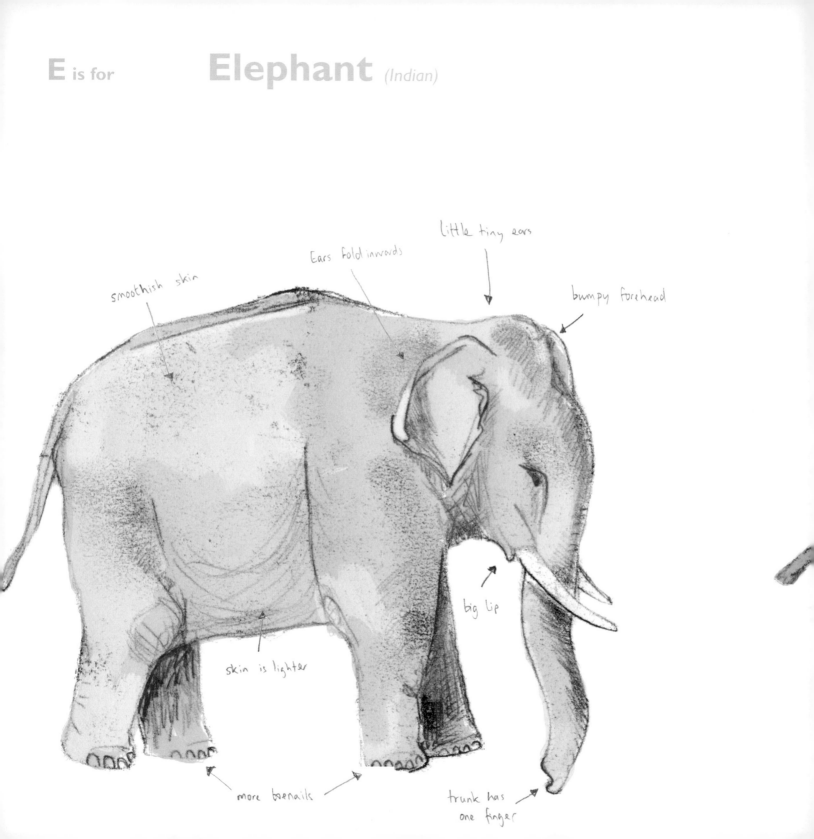

E is for   **Elephant** *(Indian)*

little tiny ears

Ears fold inwards

smoothish skin

bumpy forehead

big lip

skin is lighter

more toenails

trunk has one finger

Elephant *(African)*

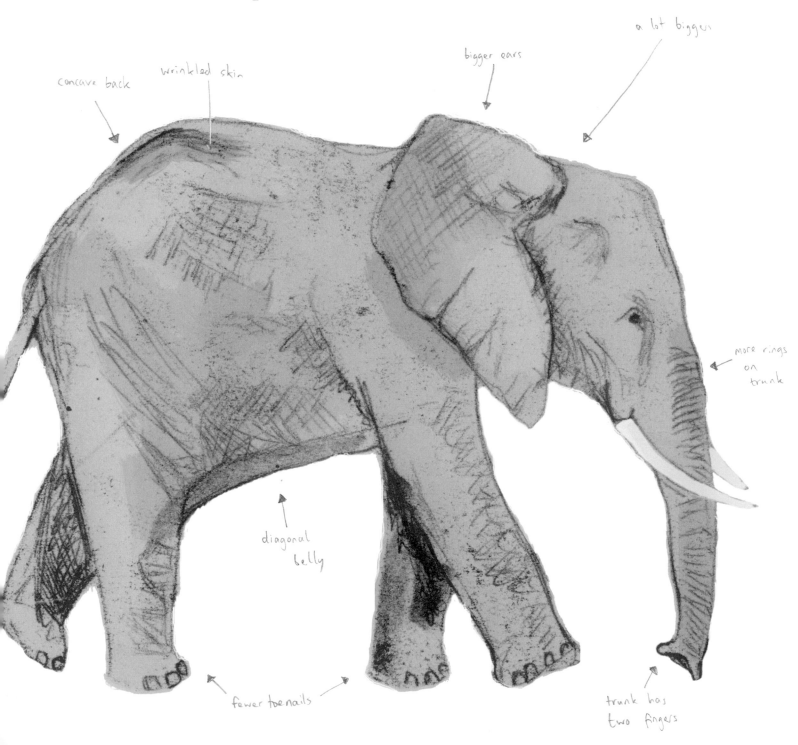

concave back

wrinkled skin

bigger ears

a lot bigger

more rings on trunk

diagonal belly

fewer toenails

trunk has two fingers

f is for **fox**

Arctic

fennec

red

Tibetan

G is for Gorilla

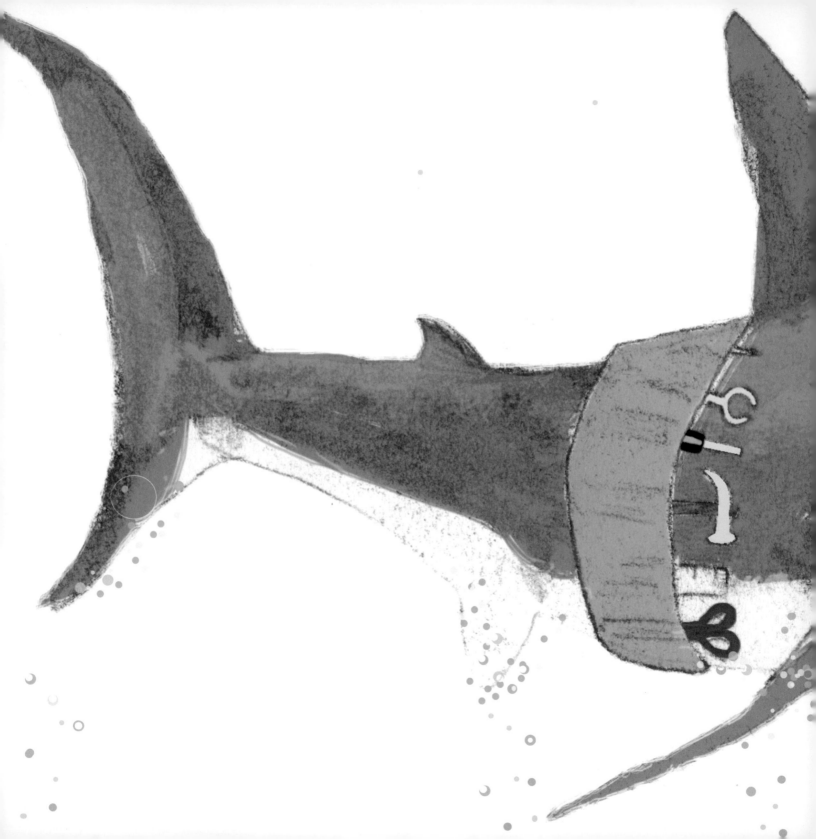

H is for
Hammerhead
Shark

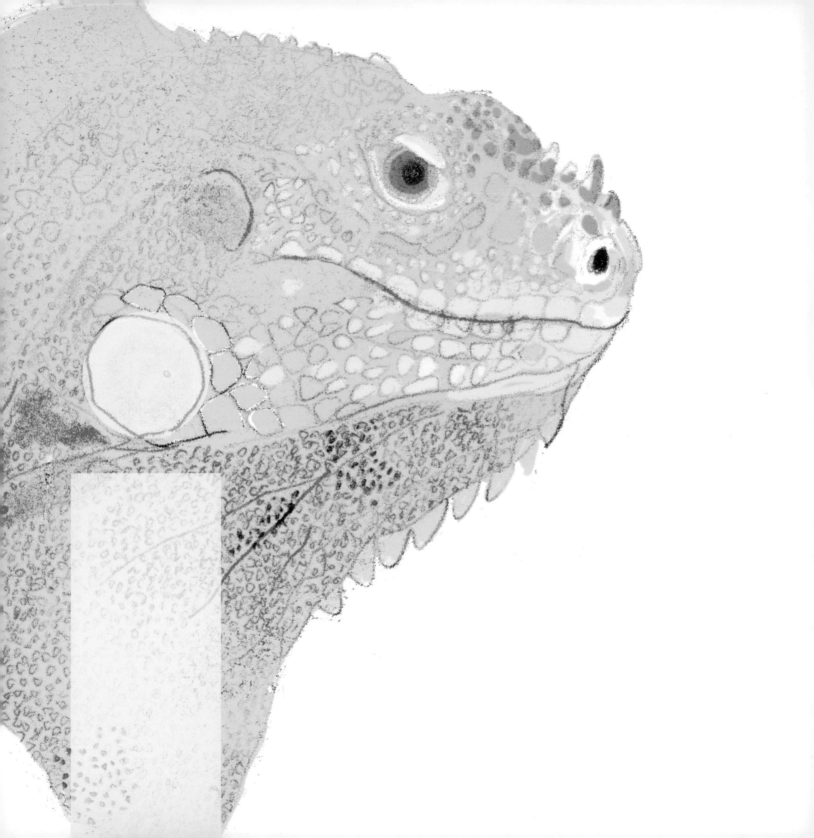

is for iguana

Is for

Jelly fish

K is for Koala

L is for Llama

capuchin

owl

colobus

spider

M

golden

mandrill

saki

is for Monkey

n is for nighttime

O is for

ornithology rocks

News

e = mc2

long-eared

spectacled

little

Owl

screech

great grey

snowy

P is for Penguins

Galapagos

little

Adélie king Fjordland rockhopper emperor

male

Q is for Quail

female

r is for **reindeer**

s is for sloth

and snail

and seriously slow

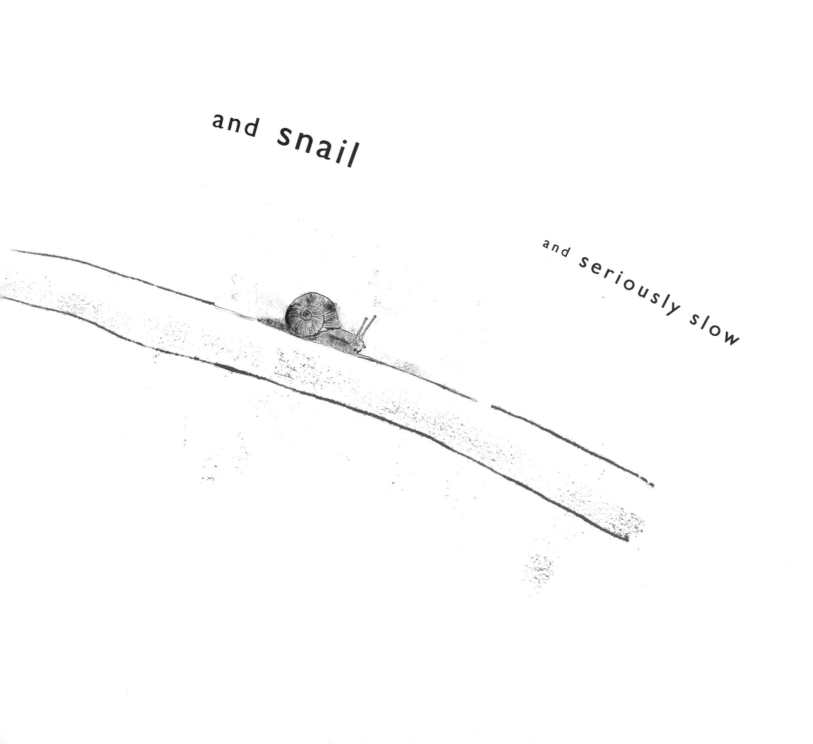

t is for tarsier

is for **Underground**

v is for

Pondicherry

hooded

vulture

king

Rüppell's

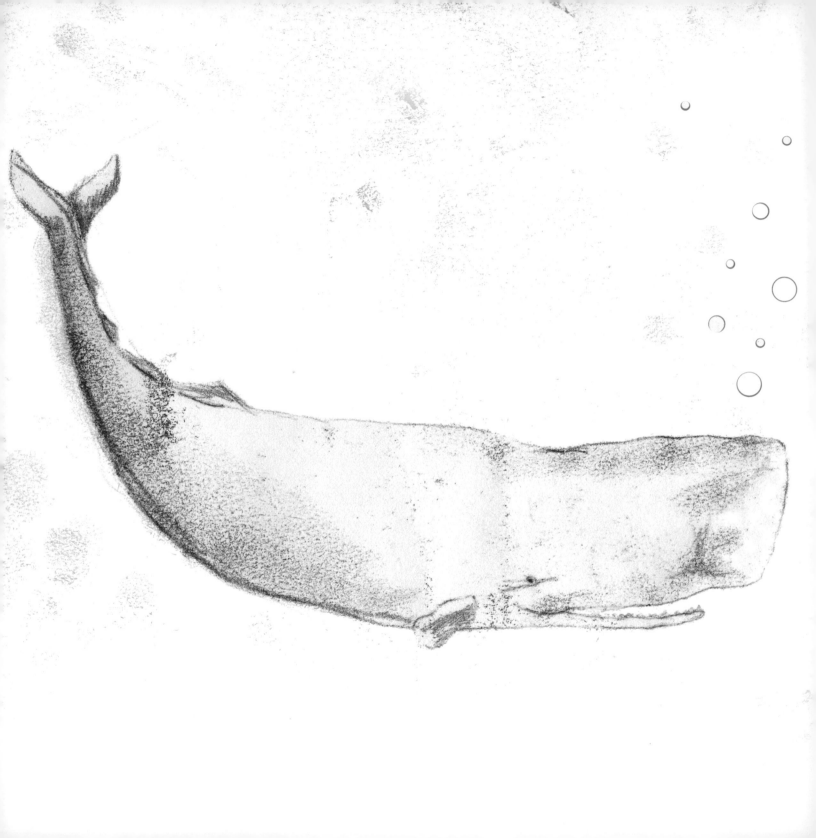

W

is for

whale

x is for x-ray

Y is for Yeti

z is for zebra

KV is for Katie Viggers

Katie wrote this book

She is an artist who lives in london, England

with her husband Nas and their cat Wally Molly

... and the red foxes!